Instructional Fair's *Addition, Subtraction, Multiplication and Division — Grade 5* is just one of a series of Basic Skills books that can be used by parents, teachers or tutors to help students master essential skills taught in the fifth grade.

This book has been designed both to instruct students and to provide them with practice in place value, addition, subtraction, multiplication and division concepts taught at the fifth grade level. Each skill/concept is presented on two pages. The first page includes step-by-step instructions and guided practice. This does not take away the need for instruction of the skill, but rather reviews the skill taught, enabling the student to work independently with examples to follow. The guided practice serves to reinforce the skill/concept before students go on to the second page. The second page features a fun type of activity and allows for independent practice. These activity pages have many formats including crossword puzzles, mazes and decoding messages. They are designed to let students have fun as they practice new mathematical skills.

Ideally, the skills/concepts presented in this book will be taught in the classroom or at home using manipulatives. Students will be better able to grasp the material with the use of concrete objects, especially if they have problems with a particular skill.

Besides teachers, tutors and parents will also find this book useful. The instructional page can be done along with the student, and the fun practice page will show that not all math homework has to be dry and boring. Some of it can actually be enjoyable!

This book covers 21 skills in place value, addition, subtraction, multiplication and division of whole numbers. The answers to the activities can be found on pages 44-48. Other books with this same format for fifth grade that you might wish to consider include *Fractions and Decimals* and *Math Topics*.

Reading and Writing Numbers

Examples

863	eight hundred sixty-three
52,032	fifty-two thousand, thirty-two
427,916	four hundred twenty-seven thousand, nine hundred sixteen
3,156,708	three million, one hundred fifty-six thousand, seven hundred eight
8,526,019,007	eight billion, five hundred twenty-six million, nineteen thousand, seven

Read and write the following numbers.

1. 430,811 _____
2. 1,987,005 _____
3. 609,832,807 _____
4. 789 _____
5. 5,476 _____
6. 6,032,019,762 _____
7. 12,543 _____

Write the numeral for the following written numbers.

8. seven billion, fifty-six million, four hundred three thousand, six hundred twenty-seven _____

9. three hundred thousand, five hundred seventy-six _____

10. twenty-six thousand, eight hundred _____

11. nine million, four hundred thirty-one thousand, five hundred ninety-four _____

12. three hundred sixteen million, forty-three thousand, one _____

13. five thousand one _____

14. six hundred thirteen thousand, one hundred sixty-five _____

Across, Down and All Around

Reading and Writing Numbers

Charm this crossnumber! Write the numeral for each of the clues.

Across

1. five hundred seventy-two
3. fifty-one thousand, one hundred twenty-six
5. eighty-nine thousand, seven hundred sixty-five
6. four hundred thirty-one
7. forty-nine
10. one thousand, nine hundred ninety-three
12. eight thousand, nine
13. seven hundred sixty-four million, three hundred-thousand, one hundred ninety-six
15. five hundred-thousand, two hundred twenty-six

Down

2. seven thousand, sixty-four
3. fifty-two thousand, seven hundred fifty-four
4. six hundred one
5. eight thousand, one hundred sixty-three
8. ninety-eight thousand, three hundred ten
9. seventy thousand one hundred sixty-one
10. fourteen million, one hundred twenty thousand, one hundred ninety
11. ninety thousand, four hundred seventy-six
14. four thousand, six hundred fifty-five

Place Value

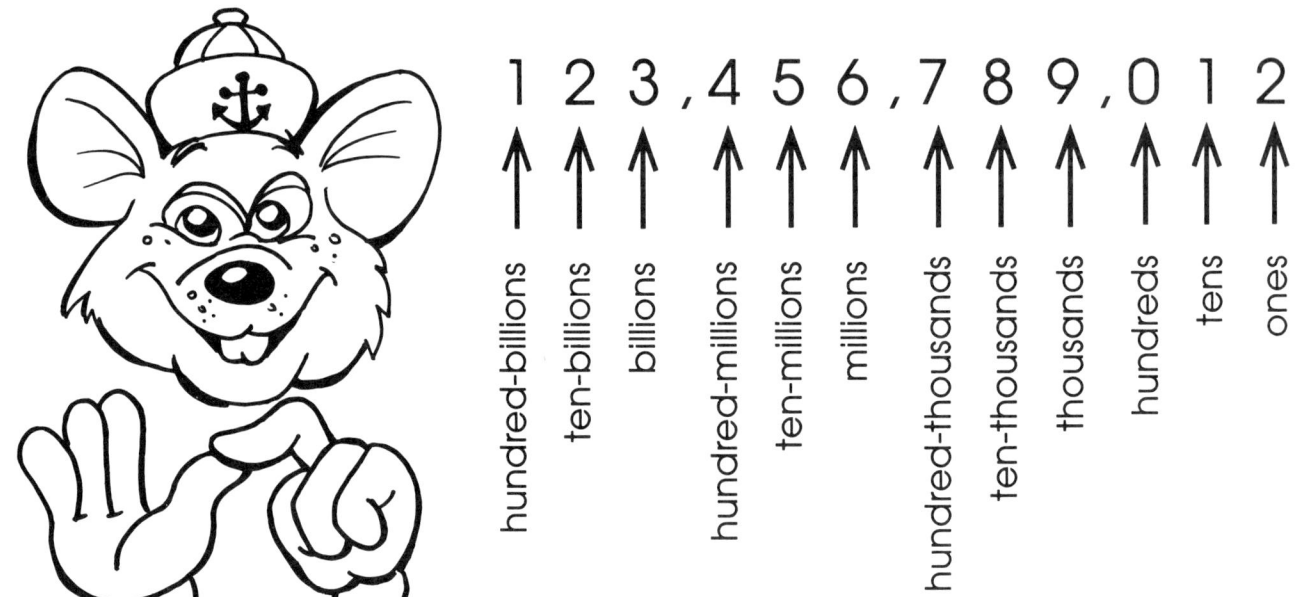

1. The number 192,647,518,209 has:

   _____ thousands   _____ ten-billions
   _____ billions   _____ millions
   _____ ten-millions   _____ hundreds
   _____ ones   _____ hundred-millions
   _____ hundred-thousands _____ ten-thousands
   _____ hundred-billions   _____ tens

2. What number has:

   5 hundred-millions   4 ones
   2 ten-thousands   6 hundred-thousands
   7 tens   5 billions
   4 hundred-billions   1 hundred
   0 thousands   9 millions
   3 ten-millions   6 ten-billions

   The number is _____

3. In the number 245,202,465,442, which places have the same numbers?

   _____

Mickey's Real Name

When Walt Disney first created Mickey Mouse, he named him something else. To find out what the name was, write the place value of the underlined number on the lines next to each number. When you are done, read the letters with the circles starting from the top.

4_6_,000,612 ◯ _____

9,40_5_ ◯ _____

3,782,7_8_0 _____ ◯ ___

668,966,0_2_4 ◯ _____

_5_1,805,421 _____ ◯ ___

_2_02,485,799 _____ ◯ ___

6,8_9_0,111 _____ ◯ ___

83,_2_00,004 _____ ◯ ___

What was Mickey's original name? _____

Place Value

Math IF5109   5   ©MCMXCIV Instructional Fair, Inc.

Rounding Whole Numbers

Round to the nearest ten.

		114	36
1.	Locate the number to the immediate right of the ten's place. (Any number to the right of this can be ignored.)	11<u>4</u>	3<u>6</u>
2.	If that number is greater than or equal to 5, the number in the ten's position is rounded up one number. If that number is less than 5, the number in the ten's position stays the same. All numbers to the right become 0's. Numbers to the left don't change.	4 < 5 so 114 = 110	6 > 5 so 36 = 40

Round to the nearest thousand.

		6,529	29,386
1.	Locate the number to the immediate right of the thousand's place. (Any number to the right of this can be ignored.)	6,<u>5</u>29	29,<u>3</u>86
2.	If that number is greater than or equal to 5, the number in the thousand's position is rounded up one number. If that number is less than 5, the number in the thousand's position stays the same. All numbers to the right become 0's. Numbers to the left don't change.	5 > 5 so 6,529 = 7,000	3 < 5 so 29,386 = 29,000

Round to the nearest ten.

1. 5,062
2. 93
3. 155

Round to the nearest hundred.

4. 444
5. 3,670
6. 188

Round to the nearest thousand.

7. 7,543
8. 12,699
9. 5,098

Ghostly Problems

Rounding Whole Numbers

What do you call a noisy ghost? Follow the directions below to find out.

1. Put an A above number 2 if 31,842 rounded to the nearest thousand is 31,000.
2. Put an E above number 8 if 62 rounded to the nearest ten is 60.
3. Put an S above number 10 if 4,234 rounded to the nearest hundred is 4,200.
4. Put an L above number 3 if 677 rounded to the nearest hundred is 700.
5. Put an E above number 5 if 345 rounded to the nearest ten is 350.

6. Put an A above number 9 if 5,499 rounded to the nearest thousand is 6,000.
7. Put a B above number 1 if 94 rounded to the nearest ten is 100.
8. Put an O above number 2 if 885 rounded to the nearest hundred is 900.
9. Put a T above number 11 if 521 rounded to the nearest ten is 520.
10. Put an R above number 6 if 76 rounded to the nearest ten is 80.

11. Put an I above number 9 if 3,291 rounded to the nearest thousand is 3,000.
12. Put a T above number 4 if 258 rounded to the nearest hundred is 300.
13. Put a T above number 7 if 615 rounded to the nearest ten is 610.
14. Put a P above number 1 if 198 rounded to the nearest hundred is 200.
15. Put a G above number 7 if 6,817 rounded to the nearest thousand is 7,000.

___ ___ ___ ___ ___ ___   ___ ___ ___ ___ ___
 1   2   3   4   5   6   7   8   9   10   11

Addition of Two Numbers

Example A (no regrouping)

```
  148
+ 231
-----
  379
```

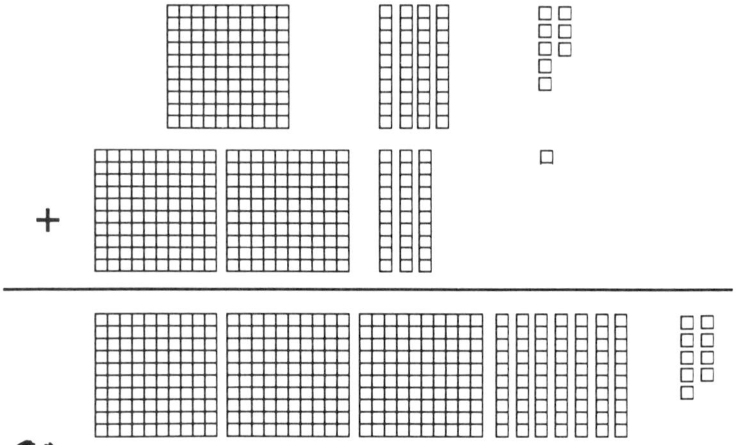

Example B (regrouping)

```
  11
  186
+  59
-----
  246
```

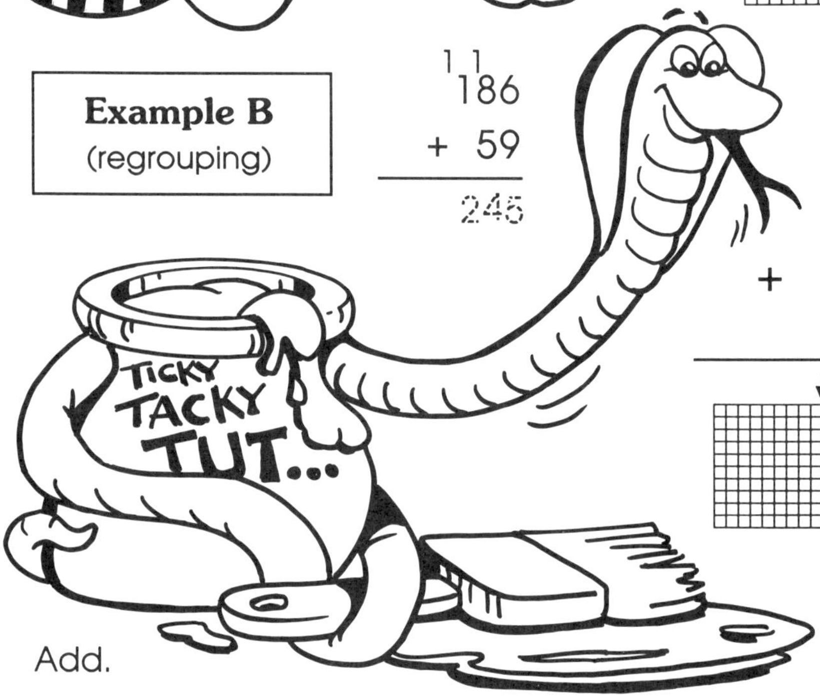

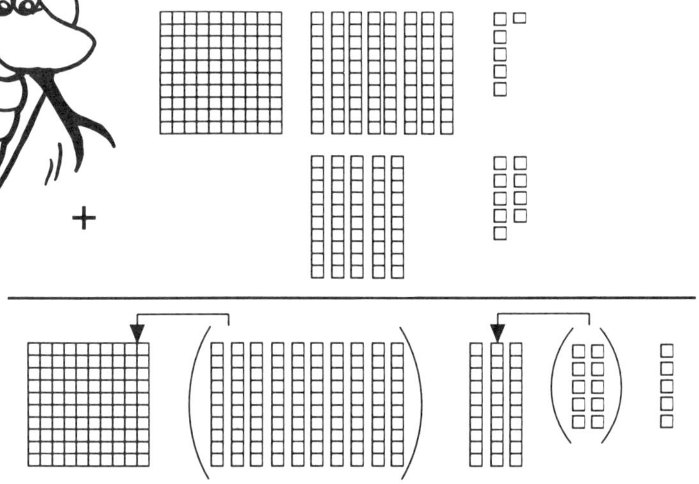

15 ones = 1 ten 5 ones
14 tens = 1 hundred 4 tens

Add.

1. 564
  + 235

2. 3,469
  +   510

3.   987
   + 468

4.   413
   + 732

5.   566
   + 637

6. 8,519
   + 989

Addition of Three Numbers

Example A

```
  1 2
  137
   28
+ 265
-----
  430
```

Example B

```
  111 11
  316,780
  678,919
+ 543,202
---------
1,538,901
```

Example C

```
    11 1
  8,017,485
      6,311
+   965,222
-----------
  8,989,018
```

20 ones = 2 tens

Add.

1. 405,688
    212,116
  + 545,799

2. 5,618,200
       97,123
  +   400,617

3.   806,420
    9,415,133
  +   2,000

4.   20,005
     67,999
   + 73,434

5. 818,919
    727,646
  + 535,000

6.   5,413
     9,788
  + 16,225

Bumbling Bob

Addition of Three Numbers

Bob, the bumbling burglar, wants to get up this fire escape to pull a heist. Solve the following addition problems and shade in the answers on the ladder. If any numbers are not shaded when all the problems have been done, Bob gets caught while going up. Some answers may not be on the ladder.

1. 986,145
    621,332
    + 200,008

2. 1,873,402
    925,666
    +   4,689

3. 506,328
    886,510
    + 342,225

4. 43,015
    2,811,604
    + 987,053

5. 18,443
    300,604
    + 999,999

6. 8,075
    14,608
    + 33,914

7. 9,162
    7,804
    + 755,122

8. 88,714
    213,653
    + 5,441,298

9. 3,244,662
    1,986,114
    + 521,387

10. 4,581
    22,983
    + 5,618,775

11. 818,623
    926
    + 3,260,004

12. 80,436
    9,159
    + 3,028,761

13. 25,004
    862,010
    +   9,302

14. 5,043,666
    4,589,771
    + 8,711,229

15. 432,188
    900,000
    + 611,042

Ladder:
- 1,319,046
- 2,803,757
- 5,743,665
- 3,118,356
- 56,597
- 4,079,553
- 1,807,485
- 2,943,230
- 18,344,666
- 1,735,063
- 5,752,163
- 896,316
- 3,841,672
- 5,646,339

Does Bob make it? _____

Addition of More Than Three Numbers

It doesn't matter how many digits each number has or how many numbers are being added — just line up numbers and start adding the one's column and work left.

```
    123
     12
     25
    164
 +  238
 ------
    562
```

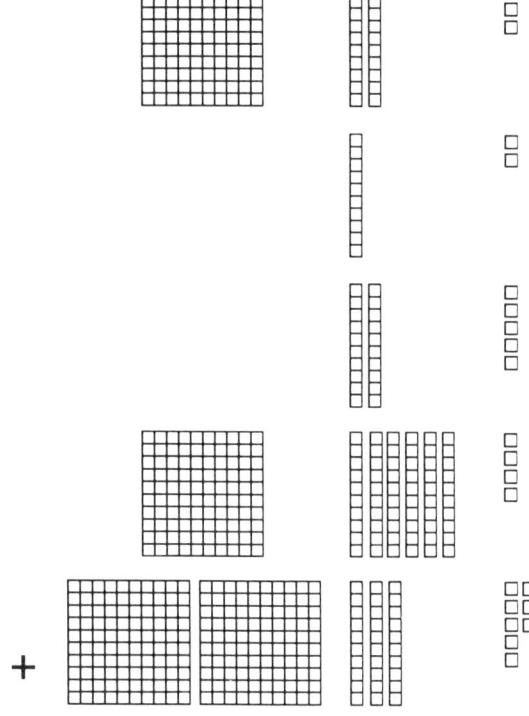

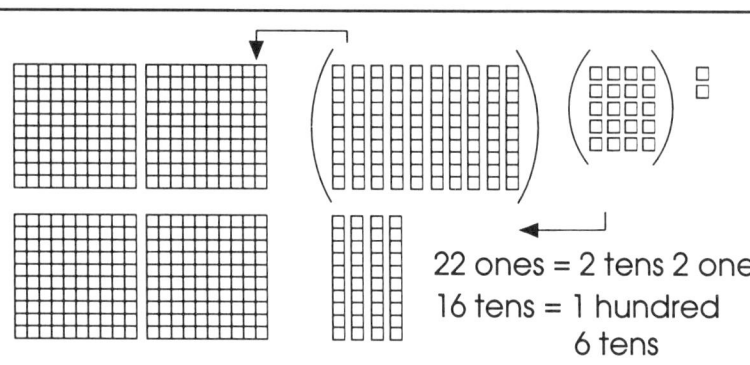

22 ones = 2 tens 2 ones
16 tens = 1 hundred 6 tens

Add.

1. 313,463
    986,112
     27,808
     16,552
 +   1,166
 ─────────

2. 4,515,780
      311,276
      400,555
       28,601
 +   479
 ──────────

3. 876,500
    413,222
    546,653
    981,111
 + 275,644
 ─────────

4. 8,300,515
      443,660
       29,772
        8,654
       30,001
 +   111,999
 ──────────

Carl Caveman's Code

Addition of More Than Three Numbers

Carl Caveman left the following addition problems on the wall of his cave for you to solve. Use this handy hieroglyphic decoder box to decipher his numbers. Give your answers in caveman numbers.

Carl's Code

✶ = 1	➡ = 6
♥ = 2	✿ = 7
▲ = 3	❦ = 8
■ = 4	★ = 9
❖ = 5	◉ = 0

Estimating Sums

To estimate, round and then add. Once you've practiced, you'll be able to do it in your head. This comes in very handy, especially if you're buying more than one item and you are not sure if you have enough money.

Nearest Ten

```
  88  →    90
+ 51  →  + 50
 139      140
```

Actual = 139
Estimated = 140
Difference = 1

Nearest Hundred

```
  244  →    200
+ 776  →  + 800
 1,020    1,000
```

Actual = 1,020
Estimated = 1,000
Difference = 20

Nearest Thousand

```
  4,566  →    5,000
+ 3,320  →  + 3,000
  7,886       8,000
```

Actual = 7,886
Estimated = 8,000
Difference = 114

When you do not have to be exact, estimating can be easy and close to the actual sum.

Add by estimating.

1.   52 → 50
      + 66 → 70

2.   618
      + 384

3.   3,477
      + 8,611

4.   44
      + 91

5.   222
      + 479

6.   1,190
      + 7,625

7.   36
      + 19

8.   566
      + 818

9.   4,533
      + 7,498

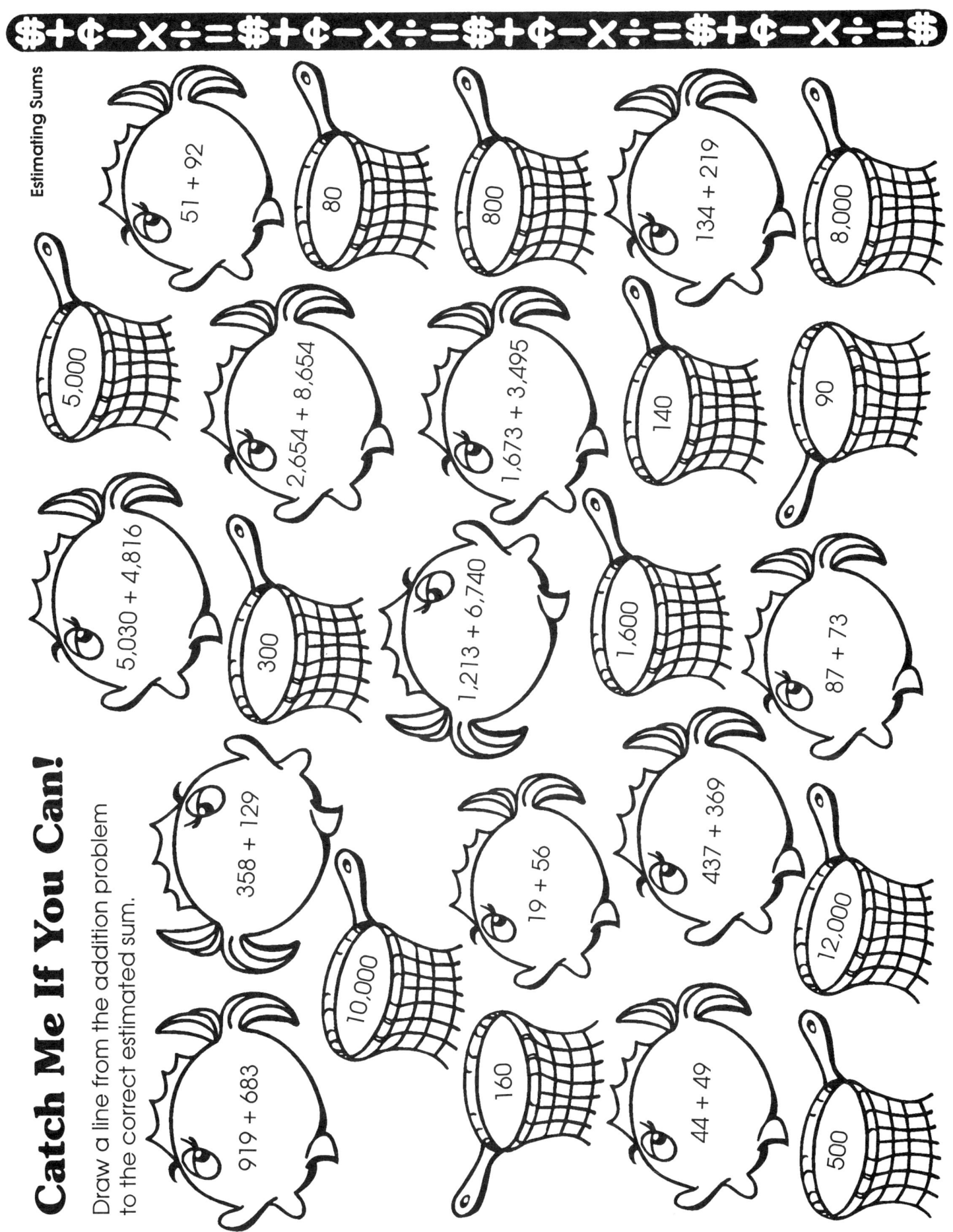

Subtraction of Three-Digit Numbers

Example A
(no regrouping)

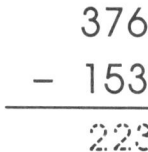

```
   376
 - 153
 -----
   223
```

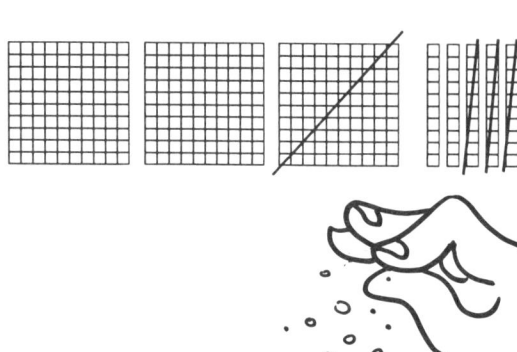

Example B
(regrouping)

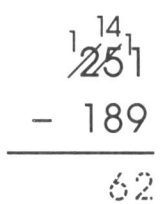

```
    1 14
   ⧸2⧸5́ 1
  - 189
  -----
     62
```

regroup

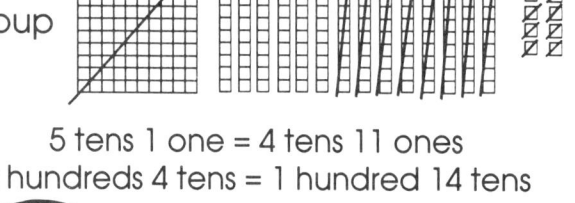

5 tens 1 one = 4 tens 11 ones
2 hundreds 4 tens = 1 hundred 14 tens

Subtract.

1. 975
  − 162

2. 842
  − 519

3. 471
  − 342

4. 645
  − 396

5. 769
  − 518

6. 758
  − 119

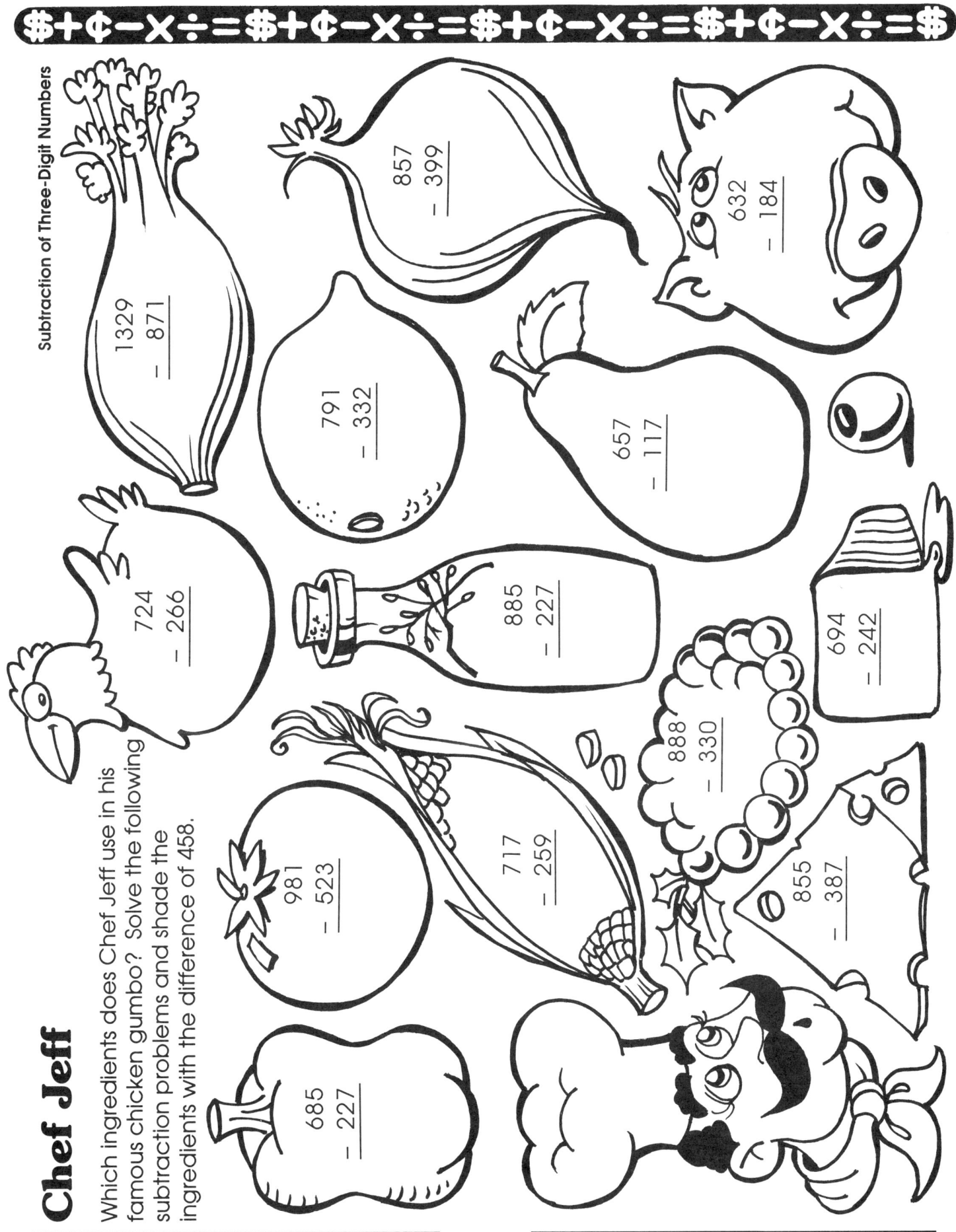

Subtraction of Greater Numbers

When subtracting numbers with many digits, subtract as usual by starting from the one's column and borrowing as needed.

Example A (no regrouping)

```
  8,746,658
-   615,432
  ─────────
  8,131,226
```

Example B (regrouping)

```
   6 10 12 11 11
    7 1 3, 2 1 4
  -   548,963
  ─────────
     164,251
```

Subtract.

1. 247,655
  − 131,444
	2. 345,221
	  − 326,788
		3. 6,543,666
		  − 4,120,005

4. 98,232
  − 17,459
	5. 551,467
	  − 320,389
		6. 726,811
		  − 600,512

7. 72,442
  − 15,999
	8. 6,233,467
	  − 94,598
		9. 989,664
		  − 111,111

TV Time

Subtraction of Greater Numbers

Tune into this crossnumber.

Across

2. 826,298
    − 358,126

5. 603,435
    − 200,874

6. 969,751
    − 400,979

9. 997,776
    − 101,223

11. 785,848
    − 785,562

12. 712,637
    − 500,963

16. 382,537
    − 339,884

17. 908,465
    − 907,731

18. 674,371
    − 574,433

19. 781,893
    − 772,896

Down

1. 595,337
    − 287,455

2. 100,915
    − 100,874

3. 999,836
    − 844,622

4. 946,116
    − 920,447

7. 528,668
    − 447,522

8. 372,818
    − 298,863

10. 675,261
    − 668,833

13. 856,673
    − 842,995

14. 107,222
    − 31,774

15. 983,529
    − 973,932

Zeros in Subtraction

Example A

```
    9
  2 ⟩1 1
  3̸ 0̸ 0
-   1 5 6
---------
    1 4 4
```

regroup

3 hundreds = 2 hundreds 10 tens
10 tens = 9 tens 10 ones

Example B

```
  3 10 12 9
    1  1 1
  4̸ 1̸,3̸ 0̸ 0̸
-    1 9,5 2 1
---------------
     2 1,7 7 9
```

Example C

```
  6 9 9 9 9 9
    1 1 1 1 1
  7̸,0̸ 0̸ 0̸,0̸ 0̸ 0̸
-     2 5 0,6 3 3
-------------------
      6,7 4 9,3 6 7
```

- Keep going to the left until you find a non-zero number to borrow from.
- The zero to the right of this becomes a 10 — so you can borrow 1.
- This may continue many times.

Subtract.

1. 150,000
    −   9,006

2. 70,022
    − 61,580

3. 11,000,000
    − 5,311,245

4. 77,600
    − 14,723

5. 900,000
    −   1,897

6. 550,000
    − 260,303

7. 38,005
    − 6,918

8. 581,083
    − 400,999

9. 6,070,466
    −   349,508

Happy Birthday!

Zeros in Subtraction

Which cartoon character turned 30 in 1990?

To find this answer, solve the following subtraction problems and find the answers in the TV set. Put the letter above the corresponding problem number at the bottom.

1. 3,000,000
   − 259,268

2. 68,200
   − 53,925

3. 900,000
   − 863,211

4. 10,000,000
   − 640,925

5. 9,900
   − 503

6. 70,027
   − 62,098

7. 80,006
   − 4,427

8. 20,000,000
   − 19,986,215

9. 19,600
   − 44

10. 700,000
    − 381,332

11. 56,004
    − 39,578

12. 80,109
    − 63,247

13. 30,200
    − 11,198

14. 500,000
    − 469,878

E = 30,122
E = 36,789
I = 75,579
O = 16,862
D = 9,359,075
F = 9,397
F = 2,740,732
L = 7,929
N = 13,785
N = 19,002
R = 14,275
S = 318,668
T = 16,426
T = 19,556

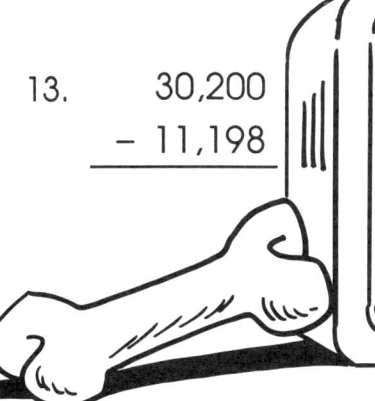

___ ___ ___ ___   ___ ___ ___   ___ ___ ___ ___ ___ ___ ___
 1   2   3   4   5   6   7   8   9   10   11   12   13   14

Estimating Differences

To estimate differences, round the numbers and then subtract. This skill can be used daily. An example of this would be when you travel by car. If you have a distance of 862 miles to travel and you've gone 381, you can round and subtract in your head — 900 – 400 is approximately 500 more miles.

Nearest Ten	**Nearest Hundred**	**Nearest Thousand**
48 → 50 – 13 → – 10 35 40	841 → 800 – 289 → – 300 552 500	6,780 → 7,000 – 1,912 → – 2,000 4,868 5,000
Actual = 35 Estimated = 40 Difference = 5	Actual = 552 Estimated = 500 Difference = 52	Actual = 4,868 Estimated = 5,000 Difference = 132

Keep in mind that these answers are approximate so this method should not be used if you want the exact answer.

Subtract by estimating.

1. 93 → 90
   – 68 → 70

2. 571
   – 139

3. 4,899
   – 1,916

4. 88
   – 19

5. 912
   – 778

6. 8,211
   – 5,928

7. 71
   – 28

8. 622
   – 266

9. 6,935
   – 2,899

Camel Trivia

Estimating Differences

What kind of camel has two humps? To find out, follow the directions below.

1. Put a C above number 3 if the estimated difference between 286 and 98 is 200.
2. Put an E above number 2 if the estimated difference between 919 and 522 is 300.
3. Put an I above number 6 if the estimated difference between 72 and 49 is 20.
4. Put an N above number 8 if the estimated difference between 88 and 23 is 70.
5. Put an O above number 7 if the estimated difference between 7,628 and 3,333 is 4,000.
6. Put a K above number 4 if the estimated difference between 618 and 285 is 400.
7. Put a T above number 5 if the estimated difference between 92 and 68 is 30.
8. Put a U above number 4 if the estimated difference between 472 and 114 is 300.
9. Put a B above number 1 if the estimated difference between 9,428 and 1,579 is 7,000.
10. Put an E above number 7 if the estimated difference between 2,910 and 1,150 is 1,000.
11. Put an S above number 5 if the estimated difference between 891 and 444 is 400.
12. Put an M above number 8 if the estimated difference between 52 and 39 is 20.
13. Put an I above number 2 if the estimated difference between 642 and 414 is 300.
14. Put an R above number 5 if the estimated difference between 8,198 and 3,926 is 4,000.
15. Put an L above number 1 if the estimated difference between 82 and 29 is 60.
16. Put a T above number 4 if the estimated difference between 673 and 348 is 400.
17. Put an A above number 7 if the estimated difference between 77 and 12 is 70.
18. Put an A above number 2 if the estimated difference between 9,249 and 1,973 is 7,000.

___ ___ ___ ___ ___ ___ ___ ___
 1   2   3   4   5   6   7   8

Addition and Subtraction

When given both addition and subtraction to solve, do the operations in order from left to right.

Example A   573 − 126 + 49 − 402

1. $5\overset{6\,1}{7}3$
    − 126
    ─────
    447

2. $4\overset{1}{4}7$
    + 49
    ─────
    496

3. 496
    − 402
    ─────
    94

So, 573 − 126 + 49 − 402 = 94

Example B   1,000 − 918 − 29 + 503 + 444

1. $\overset{0\,9\,9\,1}{1{,}000}$
    − 918
    ─────
    82

2. $\overset{7\,1}{82}$
    − 29
    ─────
    53

3. 53
    + 503
    ─────
    556

4. $\overset{1\,1}{556}$
    + 444
    ─────
    1,000

So, 1,000 − 918 − 29 + 503 + 444 = 1,000

Add and subtract.

1. 633 + 414 − 259 − 577

2. 911 + 59 + 698 − 1,015

3. 1,200 − 482 − 318 + 160 + 666

4. 29 + 58 − 61 + 89 − 16 + 35 − 34

Math IF5109

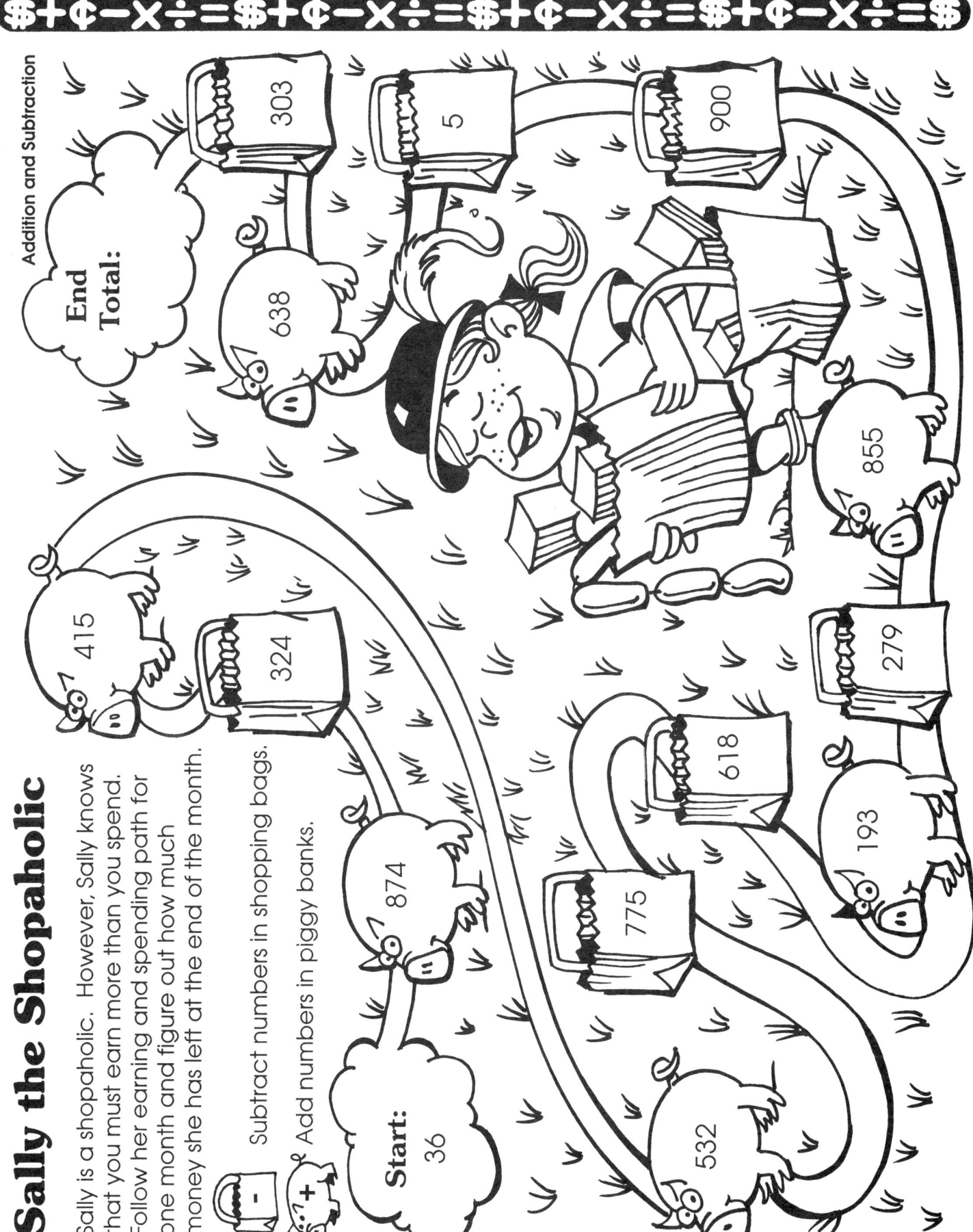

Multiplication (One-Digit Multiplier)

Example A (no regrouping)

```
  234
x   2
  468
```

Step 1 Multiply ones. 2 x 4 = 8
Step 2 Multiply tens. 2 x 3 = 6
Step 3 Multiply hundreds. 2 x 2 = 4

Example B (regrouping)

```
   2 1
   563
x    4
 2,252
```

Step 1 Multiply ones. 4 x 3 = 12 ones = 1 ten 2 ones. Carry the 1.
Step 2 Multiply tens. 4 x 6 + 1 = 25 tens = 2 hundreds 5 tens. Carry the 2.
Step 3 Multiply hundreds. 4 x 5 + 2 = 22 hundreds = 2 thousands 2 hundreds.

Example C (regrouping and zeros)

```
   7 5
  7,086
x     9
 63,774
```

Step 1 Multiply ones. 9 x 6 = 54 ones = 5 tens 4 ones. Carry the 5.
Step 2 Multiply tens. 9 x 8 + 5 = 77 tens = 7 hundreds 7 tens. Carry the 7.
Step 3 Multiply hundreds. 9 x 0 + 7 = 7 hundreds.
Step 4 Multiply thousands. 9 x 7 = 63 thousands = 6 ten-thousands 3 thousands.

Multiply.

1. 323 x 8
2. 1,132 x 2
3. 789 x 5

4. 4,008 x 7
5. 2,580 x 3
6. 888 x 6

7. 4,234 x 4
8. 589 x 9
9. 3,211 x 3

Fishy Sentences

Multiplication (One-Digit Multiplier)

743	x	7	=				
x							
8	x	111	=				
=		x					
	x	3	=				
		=		x			
			x	2	=		
				=		x	
8,916	x	4	=			6	
x		x				=	
5	x	5,002	=				
=		=					

Math IF5109   ©MCMXCIV Instructional Fair, Inc.

Multiplication (Two-Digit Multiplier)

Example A (no regrouping)

```
    21
 x  44
    84
+  840
   924
```

Step 1 Multiply by ones.
1. 4 x 1 = 4
2. 4 x 2 = 8

Step 2 Multiply by tens.
1. Add zero in one's column.
2. 4 x 1 = 4
3. 4 x 2 = 8

Step 3 Add.
1. 84 + 840 = 924

Example B (regrouping)

```
    67
 x  58
   536
+ 3350
  3,886
```

Step 1 Multiply by ones.
1. 8 x 7 = 56 (Carry the 5.)
2. 8 x 6 + 5 = 53

Step 2 Multiply by tens.
1. Add zero in one's column.
2. 5 x 7 = 35 (Carry the 3.)
3. 5 x 6 + 3 = 33

Step 3 Add.
1. 536 + 3,550 = 3,886

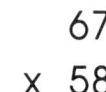

Multiply.

1. 43
  x 33

2. 55
  x 46

3. 78
  x 68

4. 39
  x 27

5. 21
  x 87

6. 77
  x 24

7. 44
  x 16

8. 80
  x 71

9. 65
  x 49

What Number Am I?

Multiplication (Two-Digit Multiplier)

Find the missing digits.

1.
```
    2□
  x 16
  ───
   144
 + 24□
 ─────
   □□4
```

2.
```
    □7
  x □7
  ───
   469
 +4020
 ─────
  □4□9
```

3.
```
    73
  x 6□
  ───
   □0
 +□380
 ─────
  4□80
```

4.
```
    7□
  x □5
  ───
   355
 +35□0
 ─────
  3□0□
```

5.
```
    □8
  x 37
  ───
   40□
 +1□40
 ─────
  2□□6
```

6.
```
    63
  x □□
  ───
   315
 +2520
 ─────
  □8□□
```

7.
```
    82
  x 3□
  ───
   7□8
 +□4□0
 ─────
  3□9□
```

8.
```
    9□
  x □6
  ───
   □58
 +1860
 ─────
  □41□
```

9.
```
    □7
  x □6
  ───
   282
 +28□0
 ─────
  □10□
```

10.
```
    7□
  x 8□
  ───
   0□
 +56□0
 ─────
  □680
```

11.
```
    □4
  x 58
  ───
   43□
 +27□0
 ─────
  □□32
```

12.
```
    77
  x □□
  ───
   462
 +308□
 ─────
  □□□2
```

13.
```
    □3
  x 5□
  ───
   186
 +46□0
 ─────
  □□3□
```

14.
```
    □0
  x □9
  ───
   720
 +24□0
 ─────
  □1□□
```

15.
```
    7□
  x 9□
  ───
   142
 +□□90
 ─────
  65□□
```

16.
```
    □8
  x 7□
  ───
   476
 +4□□0
 ─────
  □2□□
```

Multiplication (Two-Digit Multiplier)

Example A (no regrouping)

234
x 12

Step 1

```
   234
x  1(2)   ← Multiply
  468       by 2.
```

Step 2

```
   234
x  (1)2   ← Multiply
   468      by 1.
  2340    ← Write zero
            in one's
            column.
```

Step 3

```
   234
x   12
   468      ← Add.
 + 2340
  2,808
```

Example B (regrouping)

543
x 76

Step 1

```
   543
x  7(6)   ← Multiply
  3258      by 6.
```

Step 2

```
   543
x  (7)6   ← Multiply
  3258      by 7.
 38010    ← Write zero
            in one's
            column.
```

Step 3

```
    543
x    76
   3258     ← Add.
 + 38010
  41,268
```

Multiply.

1. 2311
   x 33

2. 455
   x 63

3. 816
   x 57

4. 9125
   x   28

5. 569
   x 41

6. 649
   x 29

Wah! Wah!

Multiplication (Two-Digit Multiplier)

Solve the following multiplication problems. Connect the correct problems to make the path from the baby to her bottle. Then, find the correct answers for the ones that are wrong.

- 863 × 24 = 21,712
- 904 × 93 = 85,072
- 6,520 × 74 = 582,480
- 663 × 54 = 53,802
- 392 × 28 = 11,976
- 485 × 53 = 24,605
- 199 × 98 = 19,502
- 925 × 68 = 62,900
- 566 × 74 = 41,884
- 2,576 × 92 = 236,992
- 466 × 18 = 8,388
- 4,516 × 22 = 98,352
- 5,563 × 35 = 194,705
- 719 × 82 = 69,958
- 239 × 15 = 4,585
- 1,530 × 93 = 152,290
- 534 × 34 = 28,156
- 1,344 × 49 = 65,856
- 671 × 68 = 45,628
- 793 × 81 = 64,233
- 329 × 16 = 5,624
- 861 × 57 = 50,077
- 2,316 × 27 = 62,532
- 1,524 × 43 = 65,532
- 651 × 83 = 34,738
- 4,110 × 28 = 125,080
- 819 × 76 = 52,244

Math IF5109 — 31 — ©MCMXCIV Instructional Fair, Inc.

Multiplication (Three-Digit Multiplier)

Problem
```
   359
 x 426
```

Step 1
```
   359
 x 42⑥   ← Multiply
  2154     by 6.
```

Step 2
```
   359
 x 4②6   ← Multiply
  2154     by 2.
  7180   ← Add zero in
           one's column.
```

Step 3
```
   359
 x ④26   ← Multiply
  2154     by 4.
  7180
143600   ← Add zeros in
           one's and
           ten's columns.
```

Step 4
```
     359
   x 426
    2154
    7180   ← Add.
 + 143600
  ────────
  152,934
```

Multiply.

1. 848
  x 526

2. 118
  x 245

3. 638
  x 719

4. 566
  x 483

5. 999
  x 111

6. 287
  x 560

Puzzling Crossnumber

Multiplication (Three-Digit Multiplier)

Dive into this crossnumber!

Across

1. 462 × 212
5. 234 × 101
7. 926 × 815
8. 624 × 783
11. 832 × 458
13. 336 × 817
14. 801 × 101

Down

2. 634 × 755
3. 208 × 422
4. 672 × 833
6. 547 × 900
9. 926 × 950
10. 698 × 741
12. 111 × 111

Estimating Products

Estimating products is a great skill to know because it can be very helpful when you don't have the time to multiply and you don't need an exact answer. If you didn't have a piece of paper or a calculator handy and wanted to know how much it would cost to buy a $118 bike for each of the 32 people in your class, you could estimate.

Nearest Ten

```
  81  →      80   1 zero
x 65  →    x 70   1 zero
           5,600  2 zeros
```

1. Round the numbers to be multiplied.
2. Multiply the non-zero numbers.
3. Count the number of zeros in the rounded numbers and add them to the end of the product.

Nearest Hundred

```
  544  →      500
x 655  →    x 700
          350,000
```

Nearest Hundred and Ten

```
  118  →     100
x  32  →   x  30
            3000
```

Multiply.

1. 361 → 400
    x 289 → 300

2. 85
    x 33

3. 917
    x 62

4. 191
    x 456

5. 65
    x 71

6. 834
    x 85

7. 733
    x 741

8. 59
    x 42

9. 403
    x 98

Raindrops Keep Falling

Estimating Products

Draw a line from the multiplication problem to the correct estimated product.

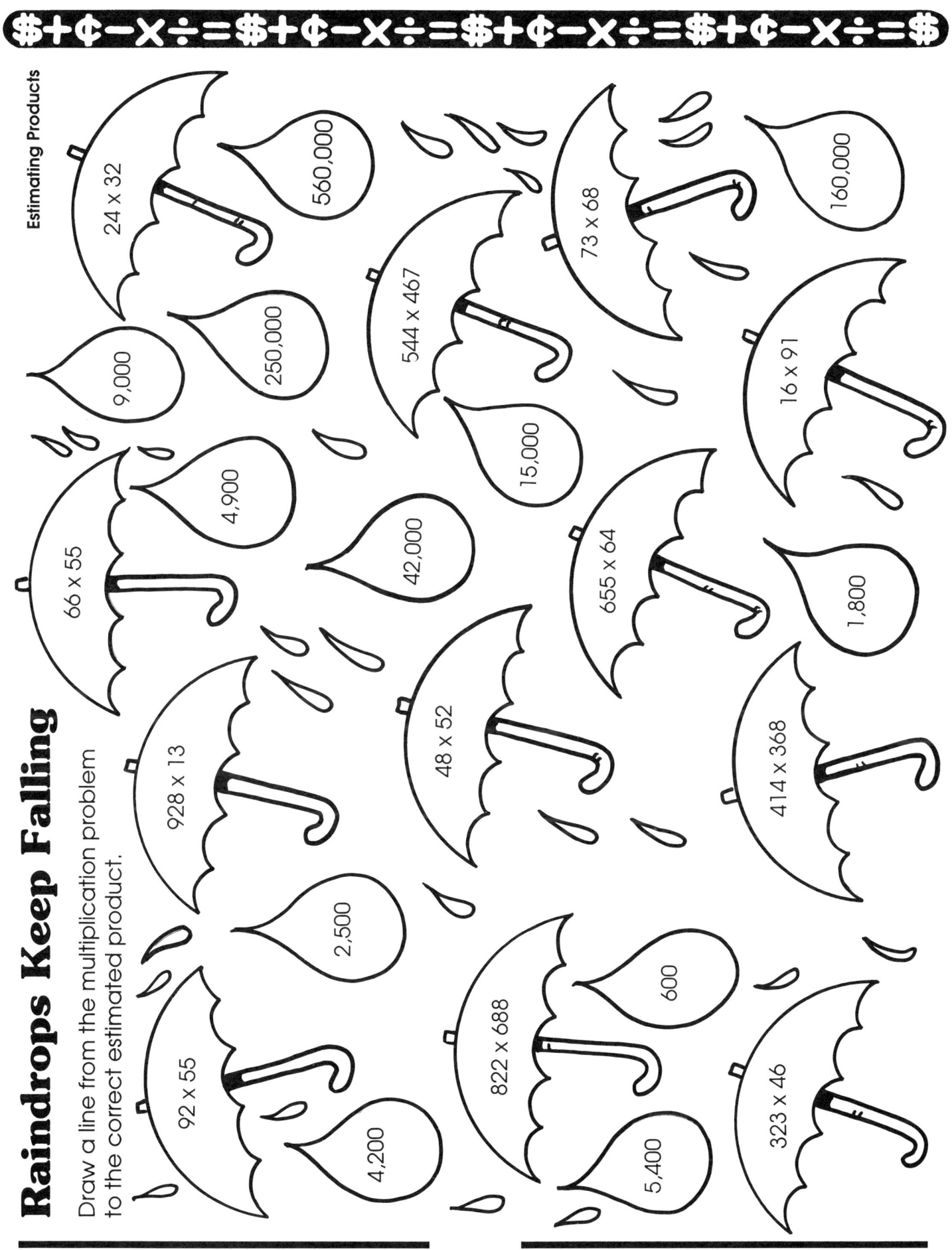

24 x 32 — 560,000
73 x 68 — 160,000
544 x 467 — 250,000
16 x 91 — 9,000
66 x 55 — 4,900
15,000
42,000
655 x 64 — 1,800
928 x 13 — 2,500
48 x 52 — 414 x 368
822 x 688 — 600
92 x 55 — 4,200
323 x 46 — 5,400

Division (One-Digit Divisor)

$435 \div 5$

$$\begin{array}{r} 8 \\ 5{\overline{\smash{\big)}\,435}} \\ -40 \\ \hline 3 \end{array}$$

$$\begin{array}{r} 87 \\ 5{\overline{\smash{\big)}\,435}} \\ -40 \\ \hline 35 \\ -35 \\ \hline 0 \end{array}$$

Step 1 Decide where to place the first digit in the quotient.
1. 5 cannot go into 4.
2. 5 can go into 43.

Step 2 Divide. Then multiply.
1. $43 \div 5 = 8$
2. $8 \times 5 = 40$

Step 3 Subtract and compare.
1. $43 - 40 = 3$
2. Is 3 less than 5? Yes.

Step 4 Bring down. Repeat the steps.
1. Bring down 5.
2. $35 \div 5 = 7$
3. $7 \times 5 = 35$
4. $35 - 35 = 0$

Step 5 Check.
1. $87 \times 5 = 435$

$1442 \div 7$

$$\begin{array}{r} 2 \\ 7{\overline{\smash{\big)}\,1442}} \\ -14 \\ \hline 0 \end{array}$$

$$\begin{array}{r} 20 \\ 7{\overline{\smash{\big)}\,1442}} \\ -14 \\ \hline 04 \\ -0 \\ \hline 4 \end{array}$$

$$\begin{array}{r} 206 \\ 7{\overline{\smash{\big)}\,1442}} \\ -14 \\ \hline 04 \\ -0 \\ \hline 42 \\ -42 \\ \hline 0 \end{array}$$

Step 1 Decide where to place the first digit in the quotient.
1. 7 cannot go into 1.
2. 7 can go into 14.

Step 2 Divide. Then multiply.
1. $14 \div 2 = 7$
2. $2 \times 7 = 14$

Step 3 Subtract and compare.
1. $14 - 14 = 0$

Step 4 Bring down. Repeat the steps.
1. Bring down 4.
2. 7 cannot go into 4.
3. $0 \times 7 = 0$
4. $4 - 0 = 4$
5. Bring down the 2.
6. $42 \div 7 = 6$
7. $6 \times 7 = 42$
8. $42 - 42 = 0$

Step 5 Check.
1. $206 \times 7 = 1,442$

Divide.

1. $8{\overline{\smash{\big)}\,2032}}$

2. $6{\overline{\smash{\big)}\,468}}$

3. $7{\overline{\smash{\big)}\,1617}}$

4. $3{\overline{\smash{\big)}\,2997}}$

5. $4{\overline{\smash{\big)}\,892}}$

6. $5{\overline{\smash{\big)}\,4020}}$

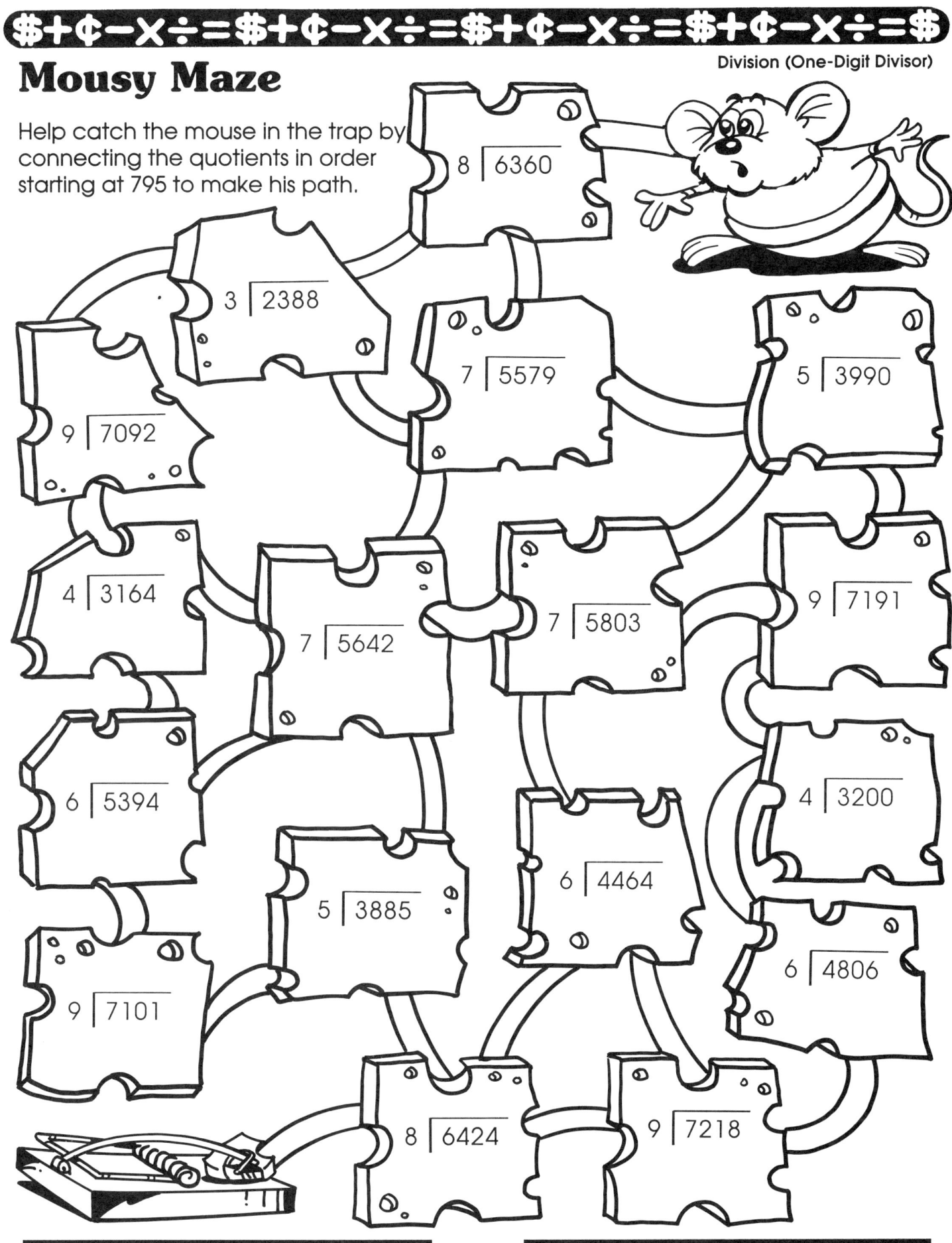

Division (Two-Digit Divisor)

Problem 2,244 ÷ 33

Step 1 Decide where to place the first digit in the quotient.
1. 33 cannot go into 2.
2. 33 cannot go into 22.
3. 33 can go into 224.

Step 2 Divide. Then multiply.
1. 224 ÷ 33 = 6
2. 6 x 33 = 198

Step 3 Subtract and compare.
1. 224 − 198 = 26
2. Is 26 less than 33? Yes.

Step 4 Bring down. Repeat the steps.
1. Bring down 4.
2. 264 ÷ 33 = 8
3. 8 x 33 = 264
4. 264 − 264 = 0

Step 5 Check.
1. 68 x 33 = 2,244

$$33\overline{)2244}$$

$$\begin{array}{r}6\\33\overline{)2244}\\-198\end{array}$$

$$\begin{array}{r}6\\33\overline{)2244}\\-198\\\hline 26\end{array}$$

$$\begin{array}{r}68\\33\overline{)2244}\\-198\\\hline 264\\-264\\\hline 0\end{array}$$

Divide.

1. $24\overline{)1296}$ 2. $18\overline{)1242}$ 3. $51\overline{)4080}$

4. $42\overline{)3150}$ 5. $38\overline{)2926}$ 6. $26\overline{)2470}$

7. $26\overline{)1144}$ 8. $62\overline{)1612}$ 9. $33\overline{)2442}$

Wisconsin's Nickname

Division (Two-Digit Divisor)

What is Wisconsin known as?

To find out, solve the division problems below. Then, find the answers at the bottom of the page and put the corresponding letter on the line above the answer.

T. 14 ⟌ 1218   E. 23 ⟌ 1633   S. 53 ⟌ 2756

A. 38 ⟌ 1596   A. 61 ⟌ 5185   E. 18 ⟌ 1764

T. 22 ⟌ 1628   R. 40 ⟌ 2520   D. 55 ⟌ 4400

G. 31 ⟌ 1364   B. 12 ⟌ 780

___ ___ ___ ___ ___ ___   ___ ___ ___ ___ ___
65   85   80   44   71   63   52   74   42   87   98

Division With Remainders

Problem

9,743 ÷ 41

```
     ___
41 )9743
```

```
      2
41 )9743
   - 82
```

```
     237 R 26
41 )9743
   - 82
     ___
     154
   - 123
     ___
      313
    - 287
     ___
       26
```

Step 1 Decide where to place the first digit in the quotient.
1. 41 cannot go into 9.
2. 41 can go into 97.

Step 2 Divide. Then multiply.
1. 97 ÷ 41 = 2
2. 41 x 2 = 82

Step 3 Subtract and compare.
1. 97 − 82 = 15
2. Is 15 less than 41? Yes.

Step 4 Bring down. Repeat the steps.
1. Bring down 4.
2. 154 ÷ 41 = 3
3. 3 x 41 = 123
4. 154 − 123 = 31
5. Bring down 3.
6. 313 ÷ 41 = 7
7. 41 x 7 = 287
8. 313 − 287 = 26
9. No more numbers to bring down, so 26 is the remainder.

Step 5 Check.
1. Multiply. 237 x 41 = 9717
2. Add remainder. 9717 + 26 = 9743

Divide.

1. 26)5436   2. 38)8045   3. 47)9812

4. 31)9983   5. 19)8650   6. 55)6471

Octopus Crossword

Division With Remainders

Try to disarm this crossword by writing in the remainders in word form.

Across

3. 23)1313
4. 41)3501
7. 18)1733
8. 35)2706
10. 64)4618
12. 51)4746
13. 70)5881
14. 32)2132

Down

1. 45)2389
2. 60)3786
3. 28)1076
4. 33)1360
5. 55)3533
6. 72)6128
9. 84)7494
11. 16)1497
12. 22)1088

Estimating Quotients

Estimating quotients is an excellent way to divide if you don't need to be exact. This would be useful if you bought a huge bag of bubblegum with 2,379 pieces in it for your family reunion and wanted to know approximately how many pieces each of your 57 cousins would get.

Example A

$2,379 \div 57 \rightarrow 2,400 \div 60$

divisor → $6\cancel{0} \overline{)24\cancel{0}0}$ ← dividend, quotient 40

1. Round the numbers at a place value that makes the division easy.
2. Divide the rounded non-zero numbers.
3. Cancel out all zeros in the divisor and the same number of zeros in the dividend.
4. Bring up any remaining zeros.

Example B

$788 \div 22 \rightarrow 800 \div 20$

$2\cancel{0} \overline{)80\cancel{0}}$ = 40

Example C

$62,873 \div 73 \rightarrow 63,000 \div 70$

$7\cancel{0} \overline{)6300\cancel{0}}$ = 900

Estimate.

1. $14,892 \div 52 \rightarrow 15,000 \div 50$

2. $1,973 \div 38$

3. $928 \div 28$

4. $28,222 \div 68$

5. $3,122 \div 29$

6. $54,109 \div 88$

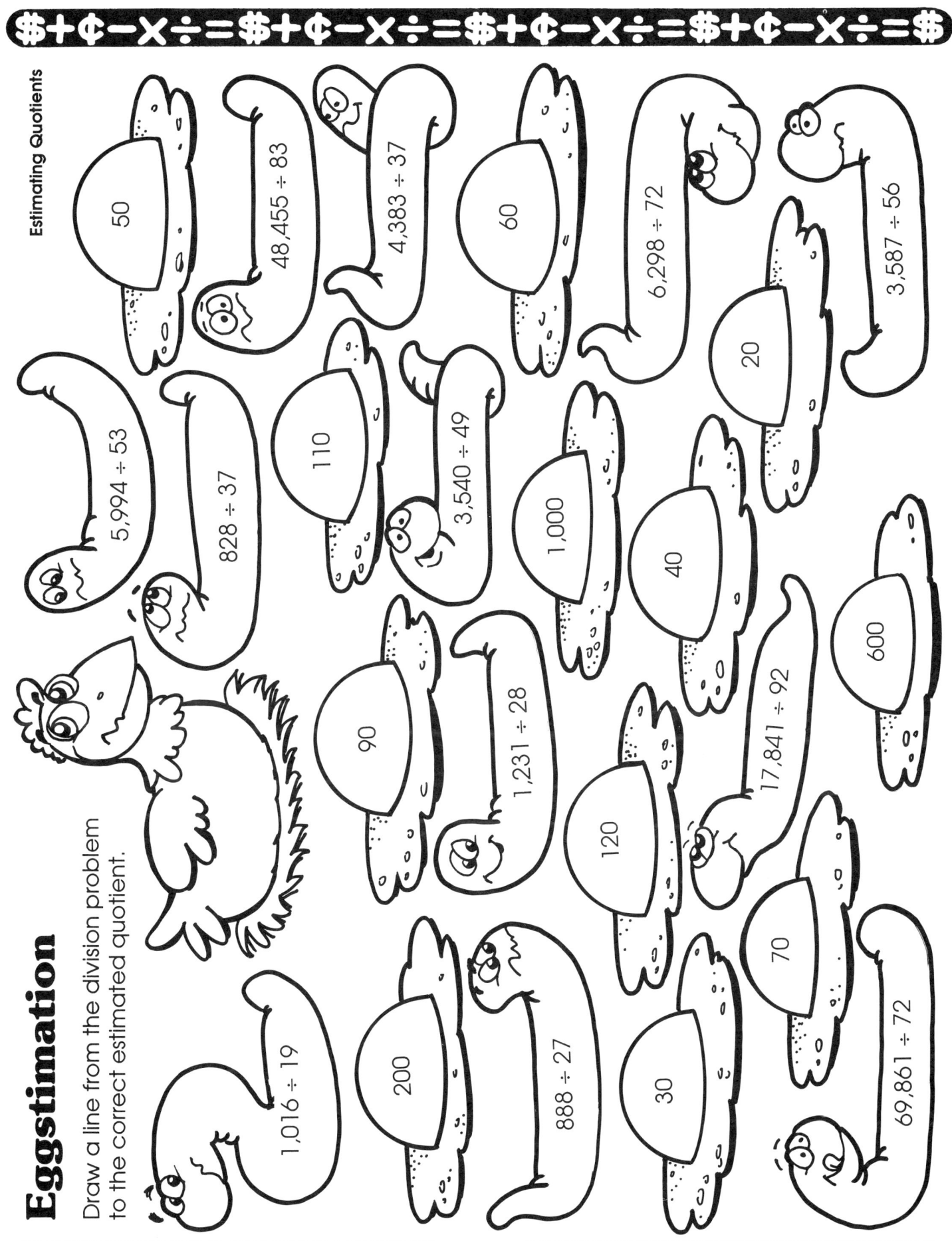

ANSWER KEY
Addition, Subtraction, Multiplication and Division
Grade 5

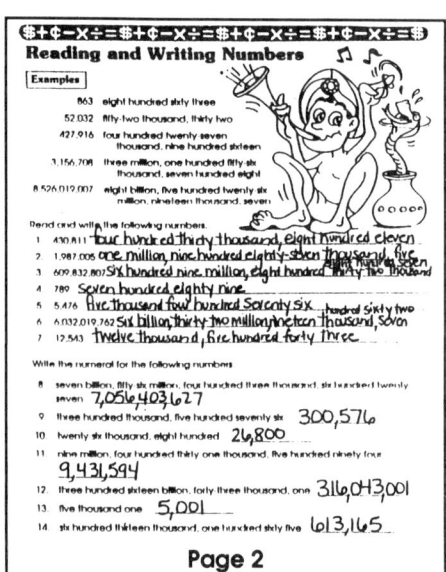

Page 2

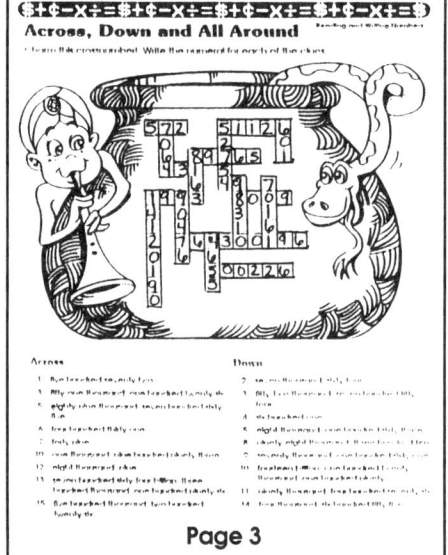

Page 3

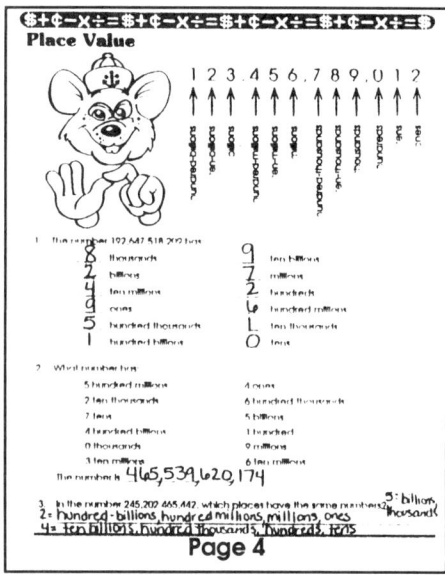

Page 4

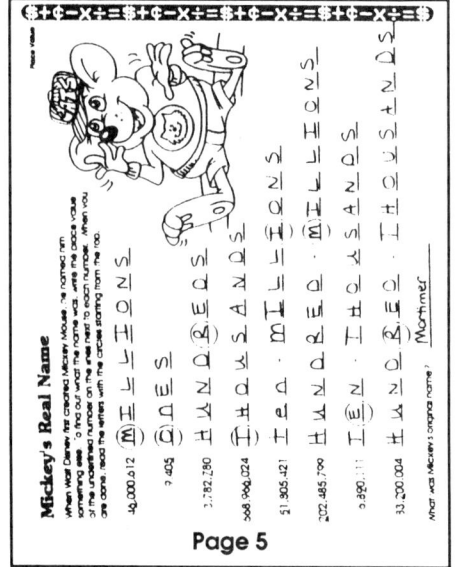

Page 5

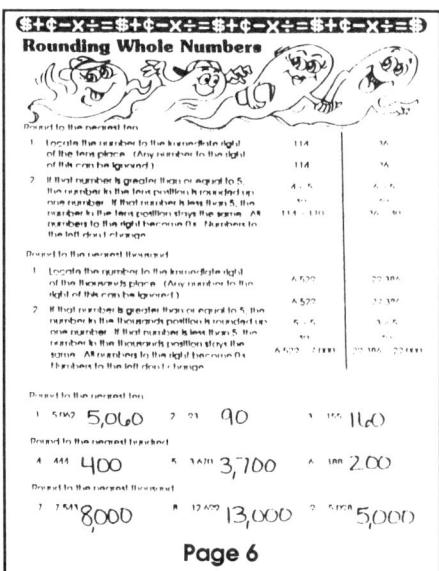

Page 6

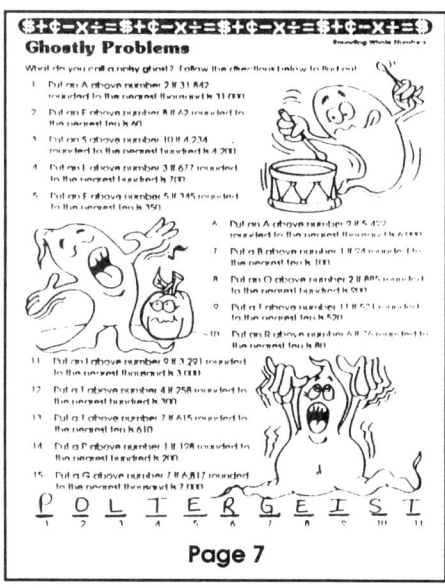

Page 7

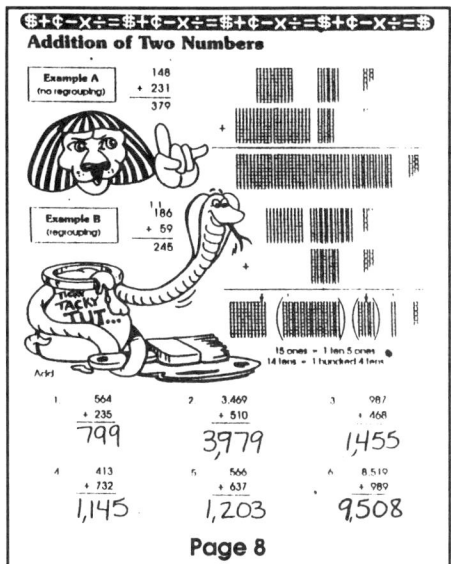
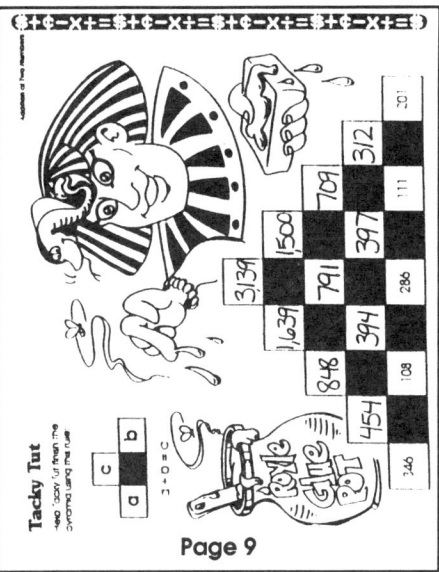
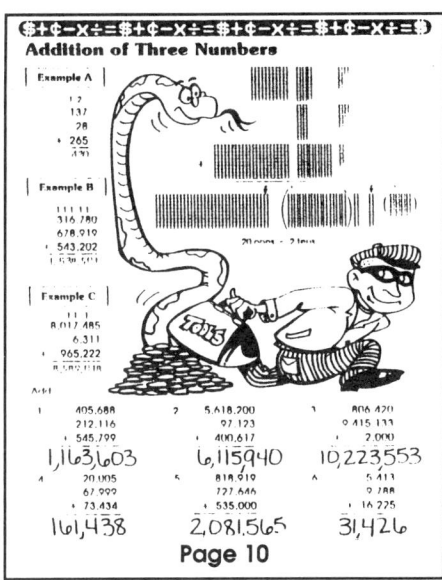
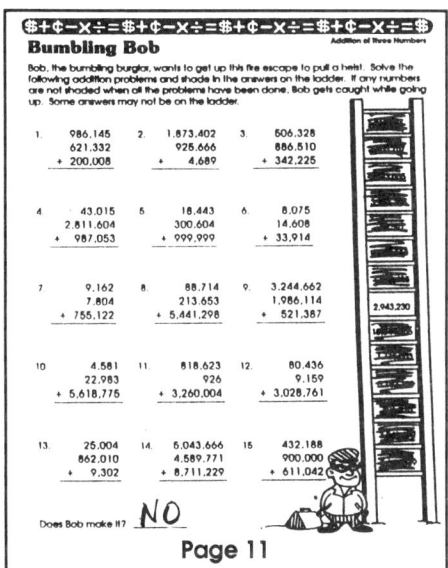
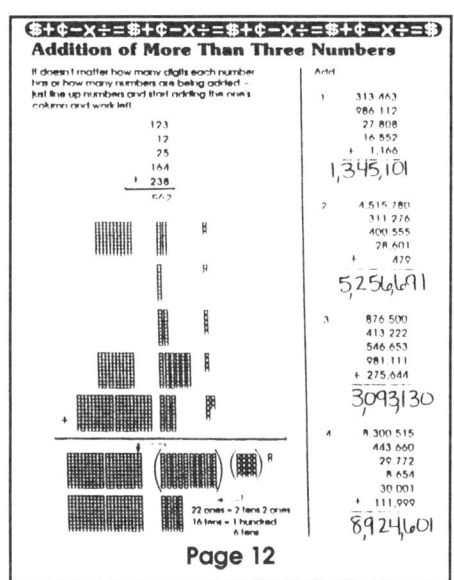
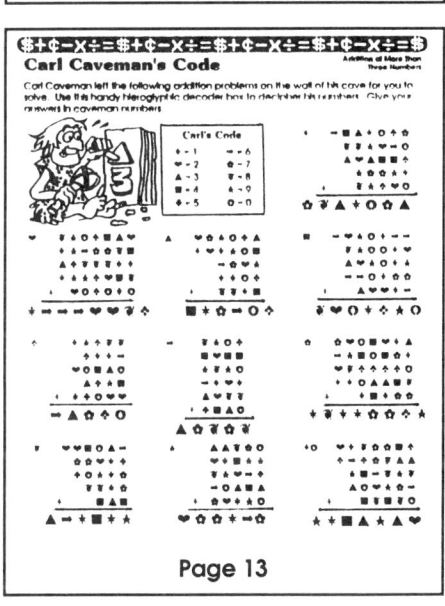
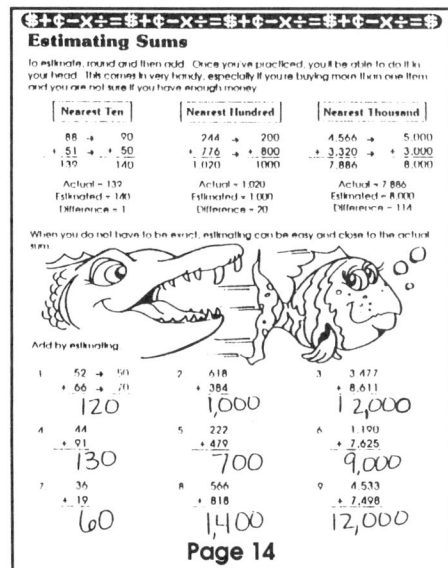
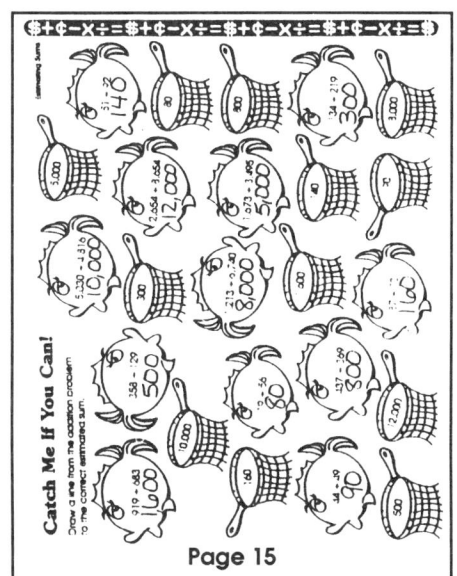
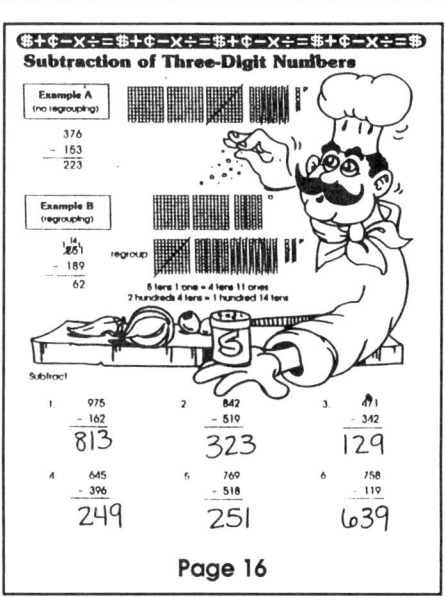

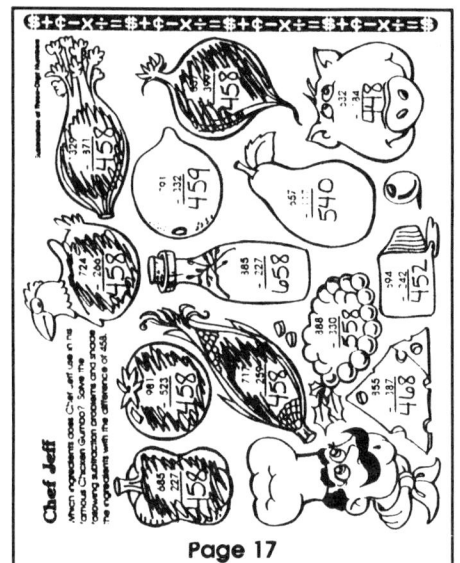
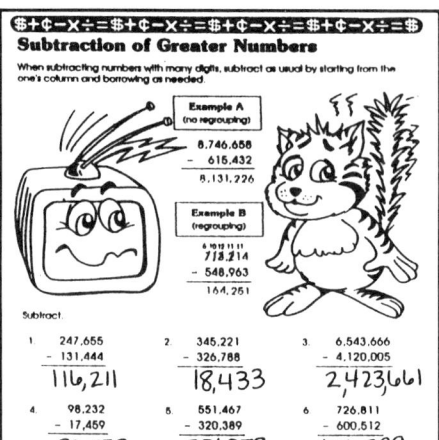
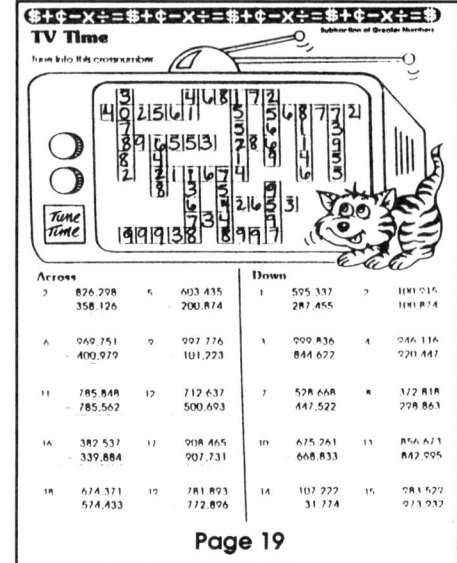
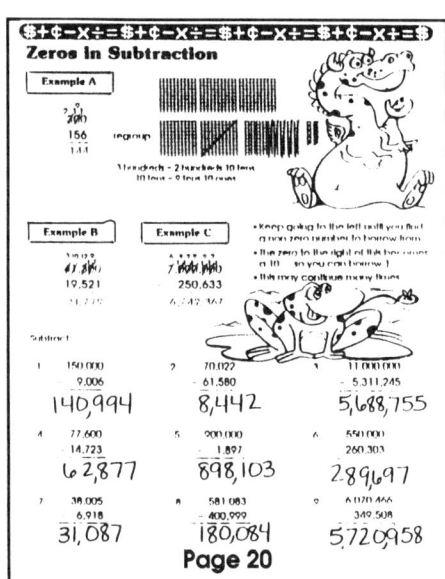
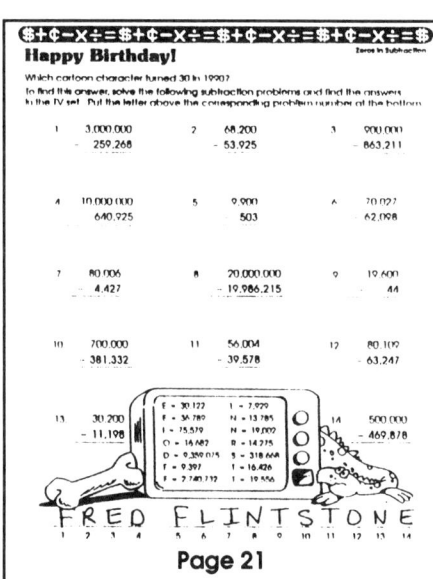
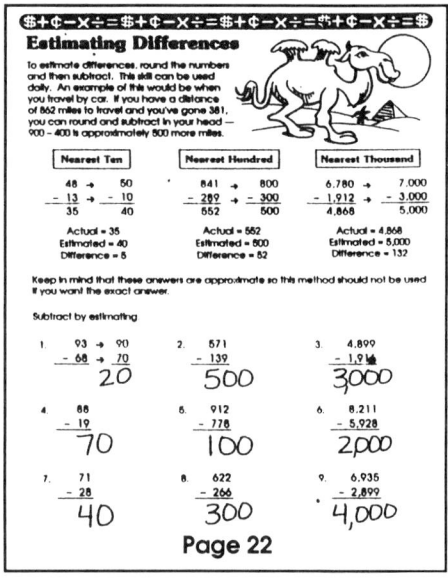
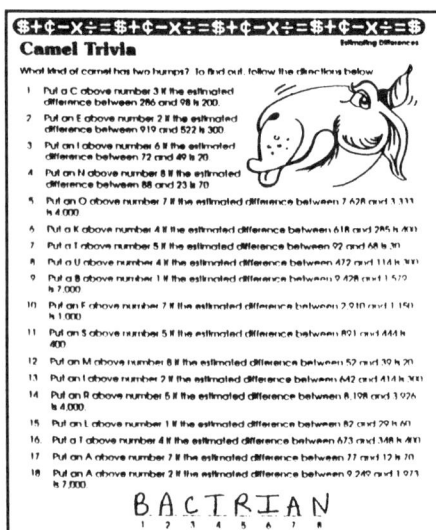
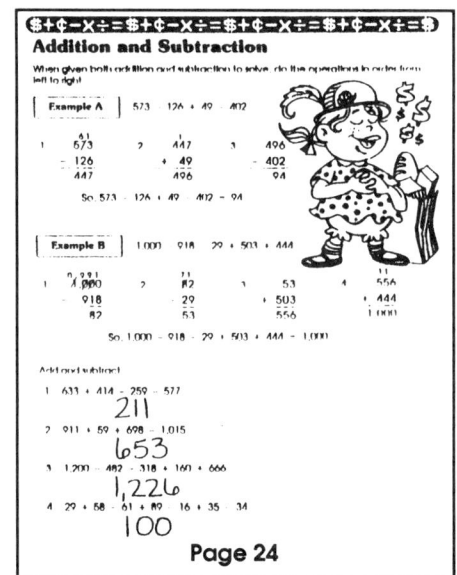
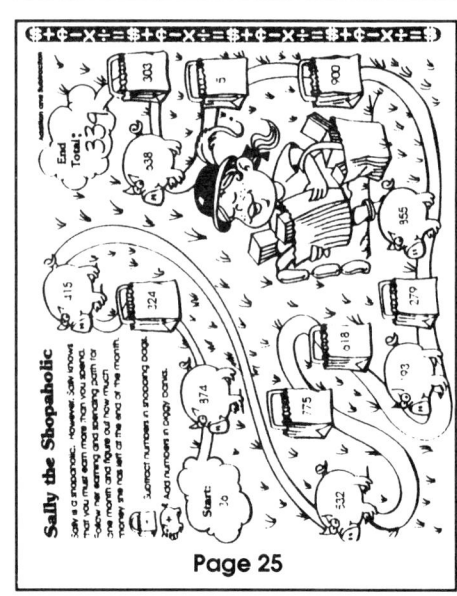

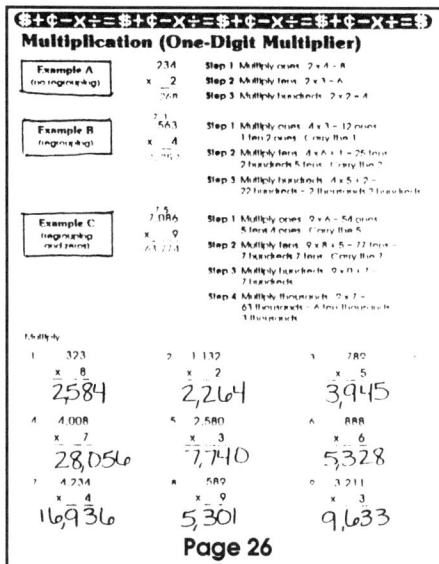
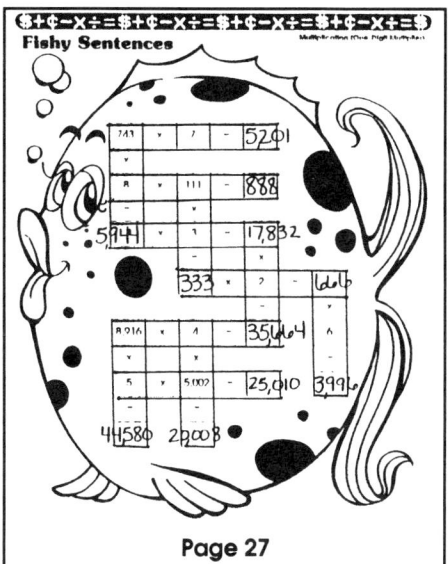
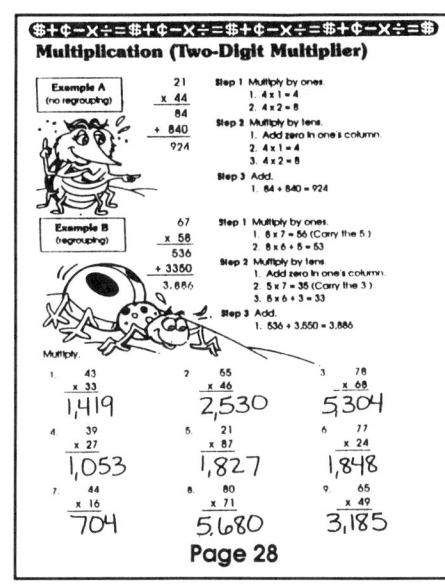
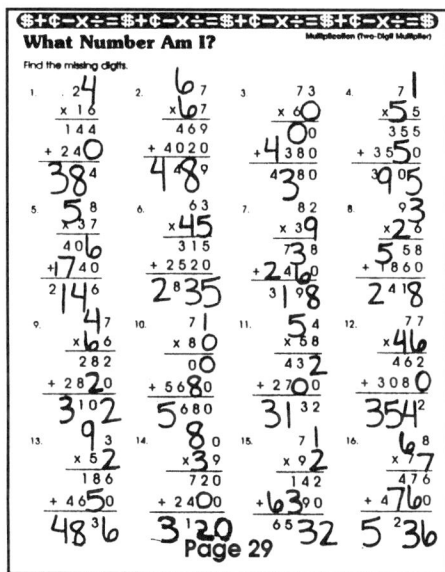
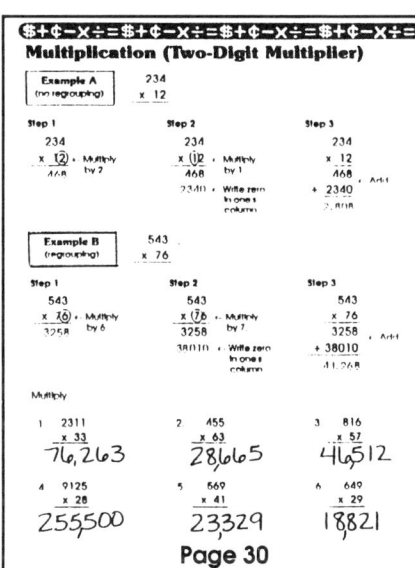
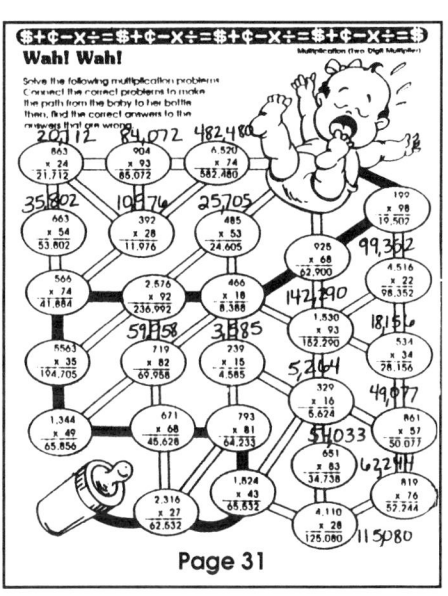
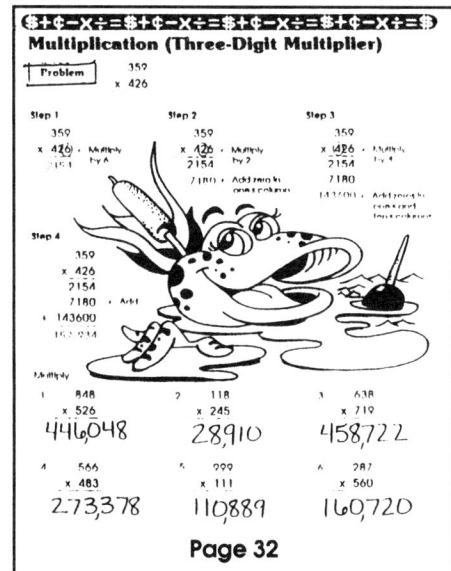
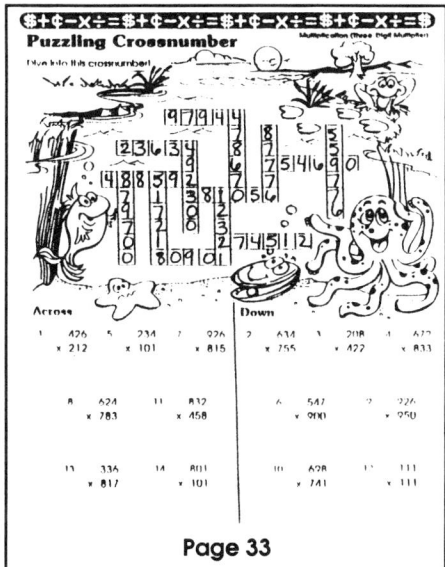
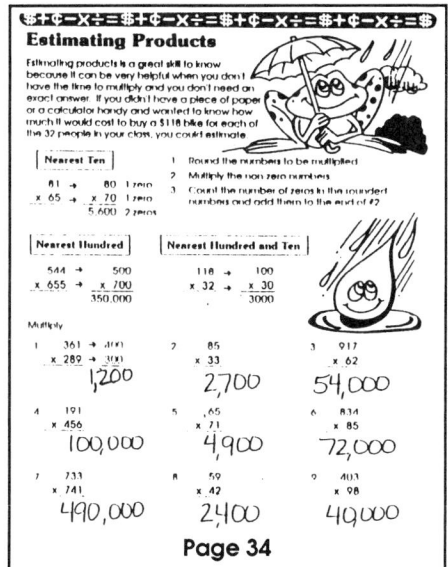

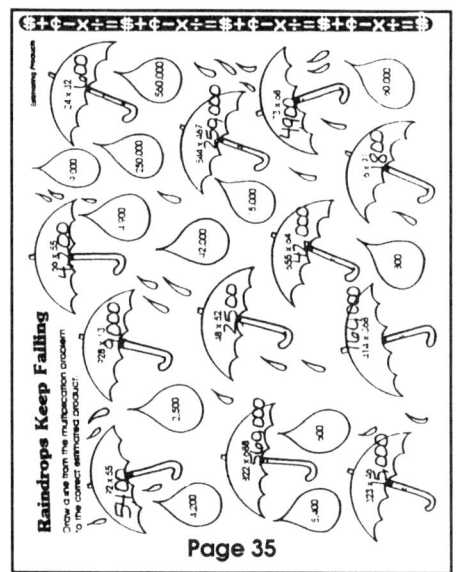
Page 35

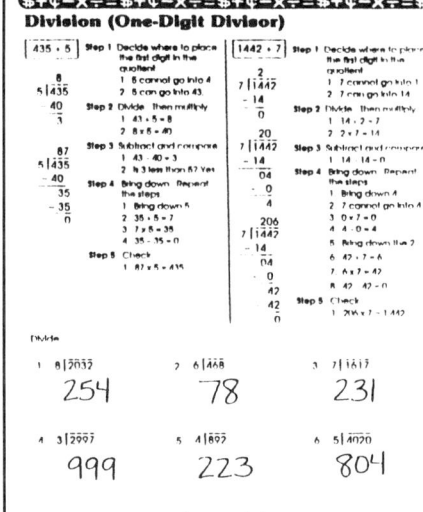
Page 36

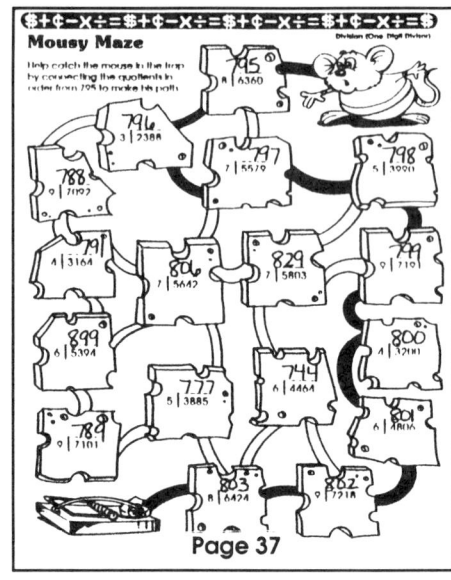
Page 37

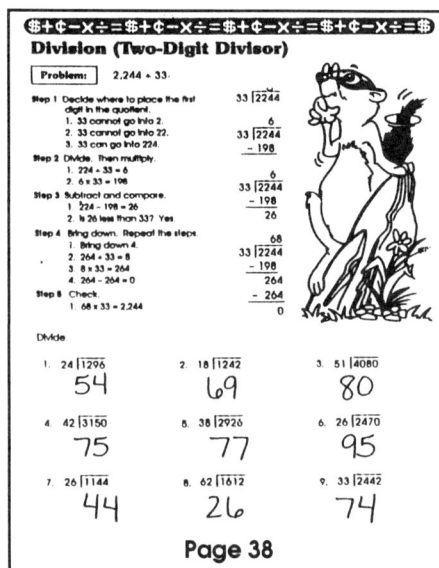
Page 38

Page 39

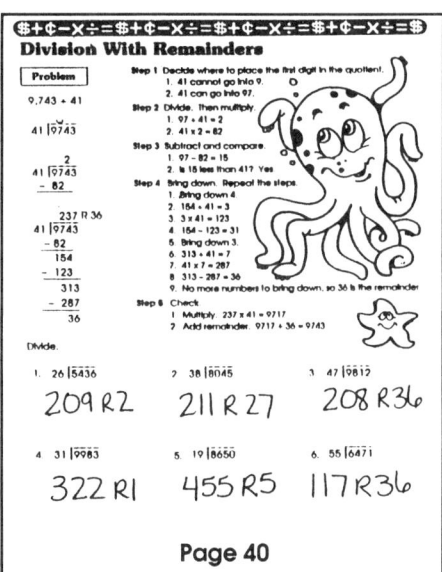
Page 40

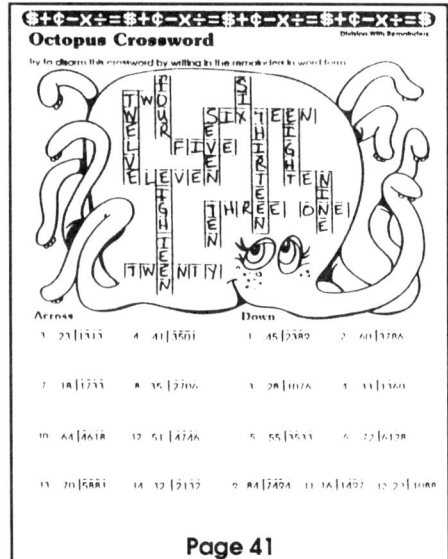
Page 41

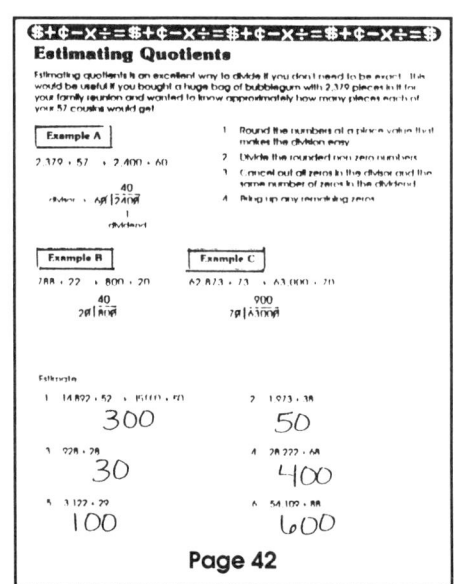
Page 42

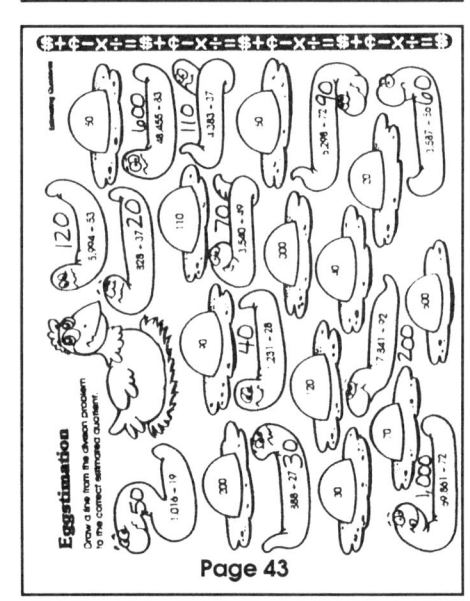
Page 43